Giant Pandas

Tom Greve

ROURKE
PUBLISHING
www.rourkepublishing.com

© 2011 Rourke Publishing LLC

www.rourkepublishing.com

PHOTO CREDITS: Cover: © diademimages; Title Page: © ondraP; Page 2, 3, 17: © Kitch Bain; Page 4: © jimkruger; Page 5, 18: © GlobalP; Page 6, 14: © GoodOlga, © jentakespictures; Page 7: © Wilburn White, © VanWyckExpress; Page 8: © genesisgraphics; Page 9: © Janos Sison; Page 10, 16: © Wikipedia; Page 11: © mtnvistalabs, © Joe_Potato; Page 12, 13: © Yuanyuan Xie; Page 19, Page Border: © Pete Niesen; Page 20-21: © John Chan; Page 22: © Alexander Muntean

Editor: Kelli L. Hicks

Cover design by Teri Intzegian
Page design by Renee Brady

Library of Congress Cataloging-in-Publication Data

McLeese, Don.
Greve, Tom.
 Giant pandas / Tom Greve.
     p. cm. -- (Eye to eye with endangered species)
 Includes bibliographical references and index.
 ISBN 978-1-61590-272-9 (Hard Cover) (alk. paper)
 ISBN 978-1-61590-512-6 (Soft Cover)
 1. Giant panda--Juvenile literature. I. Title.
 QL737.C27G7425 2011
 599.789--dc22

                                              2010010099

Rourke Publishing
Printed in the United States of America, North Mankato, Minnesota
033010
033010LP

www.rourkepublishing.com - rourke@rourkepublishing.com
Post Office Box 643328 Vero Beach, Florida 32964

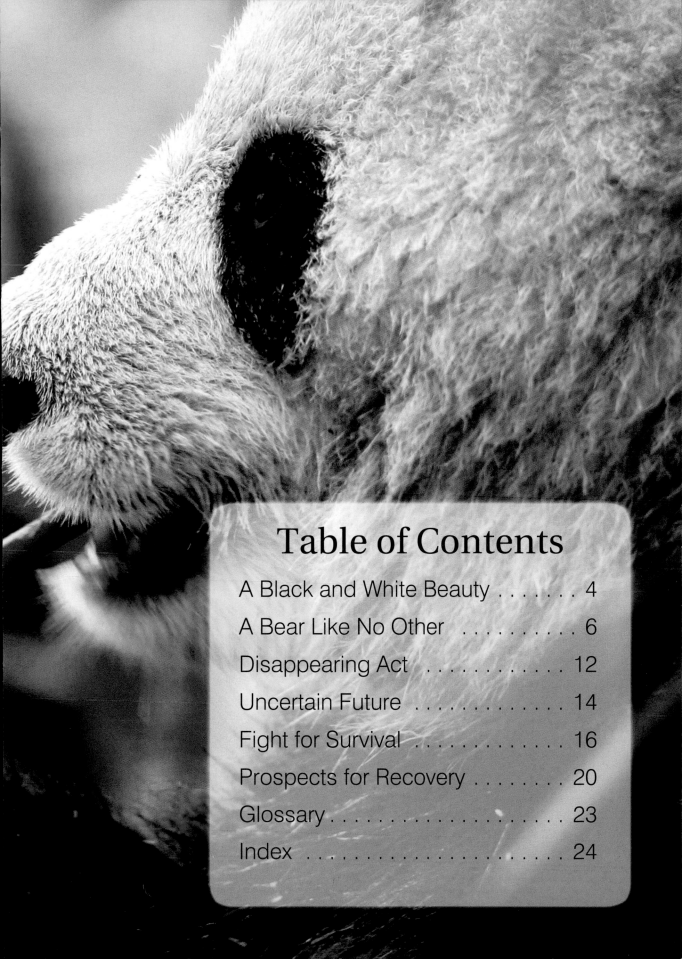

Table of Contents

Chapter 1
A Black and White Beauty

No animal in the world is more instantly recognizable than the giant panda bear. Contrasting colors make giant pandas stand out in the animal kingdom. Pandas look, eat, and act like no other animal on Earth, and they have nearly disappeared from our planet.

Giant pandas »
are comfortable on the ground, but are capable of climbing trees to find food or a place to sleep.

Giant pandas look like massive teddy bears. They have big, fuzzy heads and white fur with black patches on their ears and eyes. Their legs and shoulders are also black. »

Chapter 2

A Bear Like No Other

All bears eat meat. Once in a while giant pandas eat rodents or other small forest animals. Mostly, they eat bamboo. Bamboo is a hard, hollow plant that looks and feels like wood. It makes up 99 percent of a giant panda's diet making it almost the only thing they eat.

DID YOU KNOW?

Bamboo doesn't make a yummy snack for humans, but pandas love it. An adult giant panda can eat between 20 and 40 pounds (9-18 kilograms) of bamboo per day!

The term "giant" panda sets it apart from the smaller red panda. Giant pandas are from the same family of species which includes all types of bears. Red pandas are classified in their own species family. Red pandas more closely resemble raccoons than bears.

Pandas have a thumb-like sixth finger on their front paws. Its sole purpose is to help them grip bamboo for eating. No other kind of bear eats bamboo, and no other kind of bear has the thumb-like extra finger.

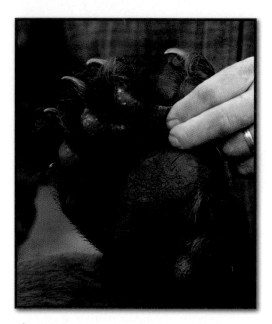

⌃⌃
A black bear's paw has 5 claws but no thumb.

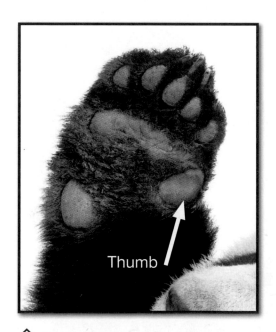

Thumb

⌃⌃
The extra part of the giant panda's paw is an extension of the wrist bone.

The panda thumb is a highly specialized trait that helps the animal survive in its bamboo forest **habitat**.

A fully grown adult giant panda can weigh between 200 and 250 pounds (91-113 kilograms). Female pandas give birth to tiny, hairless, blind babies that only weigh about

Giant Panda cubs weigh 45 kg (99.2 pounds) at one year, and live with their mothers until they are 18 months to two years old.

5 ounces (0.14 kilograms). The baby panda is roughly the size of a stick of butter. The babies, known as cubs, eat by nursing from their mother. But by one year of age, they have teeth and can eat solid food.

︽

Panda cubs are 1/900th the size of their mother. The difference in size is greater than almost any other land mammal on Earth.

Size of a Newborn Giant Panda

At 4 ¾ inches (12 centimeters), a newborn giant panda is about the same size as a stick of butter.

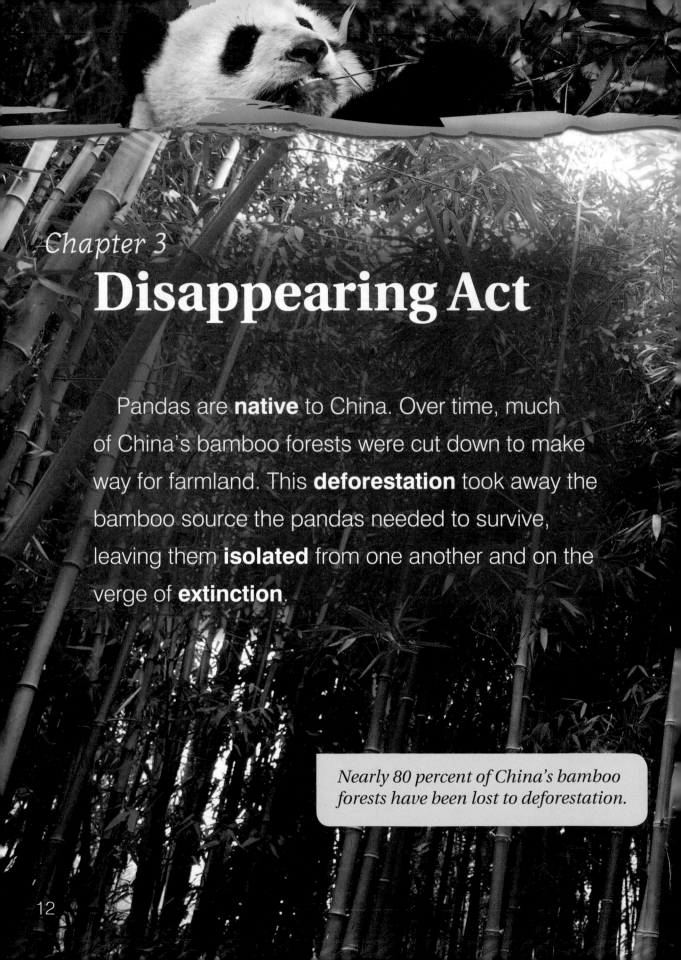

Chapter 3
Disappearing Act

Pandas are **native** to China. Over time, much of China's bamboo forests were cut down to make way for farmland. This **deforestation** took away the bamboo source the pandas needed to survive, leaving them **isolated** from one another and on the verge of **extinction**.

Nearly 80 percent of China's bamboo forests have been lost to deforestation.

Panda bears without massive bamboo forests are a little like fish without water. In both cases, the animal depends on its habitat for survival. Without a plentiful supply of bamboo, giant pandas starve.

Chapter 4
Uncertain Future

There are less than 2,000 giant pandas living in the wild. The few wild pandas left live in **clusters** high in the mountainous bamboo forests of central China. With its thick fur and specialized claws and teeth, the panda is ideally suited for the cool, wet, and foggy conditions of China's remaining mountain forests.

The giant panda is China's national animal. It is to China what the bald eagle is to the United States. ≫

Giant Panda Territories in China

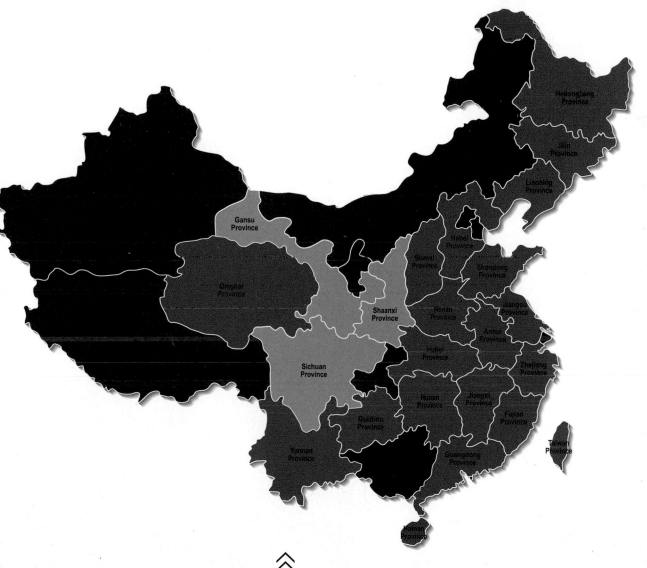

Once plentiful across most of China, giant pandas now live in just three provinces.

Giant Panda Range

Provinces Occupied by Giant Panda

Chapter 5
Fight for Survival

Scientists and animal experts are trying to protect the remaining wild giant pandas. China's government has created dozens of reserves and breeding centers to help **captive** pandas have babies. The breeding centers are meant to help restore the wild panda population.

DID YOU KNOW?

A major **earthquake** struck China in 2008. At least one giant panda died. Nearly all of Wolong's giant pandas had to be **relocated** for a time.

Many giant panda houses were damaged in the 2008 Sichuan earthquake.

Places like the Wolong Panda Reserve allow tourists to see the rare animal in its natural habitat.

Female giant pandas have difficulty getting **pregnant**. Scientists at zoos and breeding centers use special methods to help females **conceive**.

DID YOU KNOW?

In 2006, a mother named MeiMei gave birth to twin giant pandas in a Japanese Zoo.

Female pandas can have babies when they are as young as 4 years old until they are about 20. ≫

Good News: In 2006, more than 30 giant pandas were born in breeding centers and zoos worldwide. That's the largest number of captive giant panda births for any year on record.

Chapter 6
Prospects For Recovery

Because humans have destroyed so much of the giant panda's habitat, the bears are struggling to survive. Slow rates of **reproduction** mean the **species** will remain endangered for a long time.

DID YOU KNOW

Captive giant pandas in China can live as long as 35 years. Scientists think pandas generally do not live as long in the wild.

Giant pandas fascinate people. Yet, the animals are in a fight for survival. It's up to humans to protect the precious few that remain. China's government loans panda bears to zoos around the world, including four American zoos. This *panda diplomacy* helps educate people about the fragile status of the few giant pandas still living on Earth.

GLOSSARY

captive (KAP-tiv): kept in a protective pen or space

clusters (KLUHSS-turz): a group of things living together in a single area

conceive (kuhn-SEEV): when an unborn baby animal starts growing inside its mother

deforestation (dee-for-ist-TAY-shun): systematic removal of trees from a large piece of land

earthquake (URTH-kwayk): a sudden, violent shaking of the ground

extinction (ek-STINGKT-shun): when an animal dies out and there are no more left living

habitat (HAB-uh-tat): the place and natural conditions where an animal lives

isolated (EYE-suh-late-ed): kept separate and without contact from others

native (NAY-tiv): an animal that originally lived in a certain place

pregnant (PREG-nuhnt): when a female has a baby growing inside her

relocated (ree-LOH-kay-ted): moved from one place to another

reproduction (ree-pruh-DUHK-shun): the process of having babies

species (SPEE-seez): a group of related animals

23

Index

Websites to Visit

nationalzoo.si.edu/Animals/GiantPandas/PandaFacts/default.cfm

www.worldwildlife.org/species/finder/giantpanda/panda.html

www.travelchinaguide.com/attraction/sichuan/chengdu/wolong.htm

www.chinagiantpanda.com/pandanews.htm

www.pbs.org/wnet/wideangle/episodes/burning-season/photo-essay-

endangered-animals-in-the-worlds-forests/1819/

About the Author

Tom Greve lives in Chicago with his wife and two children. They are frequent visitors to the Lincoln Park Zoo, where they love to look at bears of all kinds.